15⁰⁰

PARIS

MARTIN HÜRLIMANN

PARIS

with 98 photogravure plates
10 colour plates

THAMES AND HUDSON · LONDON

First published 1954
Revised edition enlarged 1971
© 1969 Atlantis Verlag AG, Zürich
English translation © 1971 Thames and Hudson Ltd, London

Printed in Great Britain by Jarrold and Sons Ltd, Norwich
Monochrome gravure plates printed in France
Colour plates printed in Switzerland
ISBN 0 500 24081 7

Seal of the City of Paris of 1200

Contents

Sources of Illustrations

The pictures in the text were taken from the following works:
A. de Coetlogon, *Les Armoiries de la ville de Paris* (Paris 1874): pages 7, 22, 37, 38, 42, 52, 102, 141
Atlas des anciens plans de Paris (Paris 1880): pages 8, 11, 19, 21, 72, 122
Tableau historique et pittoresque de Paris, vol. III (Paris 1811): pages 24, 31, 111, 112, 132
Le Diable à Paris, with essays by Gavarni, Grandville and others (Paris 1868): pages 36, 82
Le Rouge, *Curiosités de Paris* (Paris 1778): pages 51, 62, 91

The River

Paris is a riverside town: *rive gauche, rive droite* – thus concisely does she orientate herself. For the Seine does not skirt the city as the Danube does Vienna, it flows right through the middle. Between the network of buildings intersected by lengthy Boulevards and star-shaped Squares, it winds in quiet dignity. For centuries past industrial development has kept the two halves balanced, as has the predilection of poets and artists. The city seal portrays a ship – it is a proud vessel, such as sailed the seas but is hardly likely ever to have come so far up the Seine. There may be an element of coquetry in the pride with which Paris describes herself as a port – for us it is equally a genial symbol for this greatest of world marts for spiritual wares.

Oldest of the capital's thoroughfares, the river carries boats and barges through the heart of the Ile-de-France, through the heart of France. This city, where civilization and the rational outlook have won their greatest triumphs, has preserved its bonds with nature, as few others have done; the ripple of the waters, the clouds drifting over, the play of light changing with the rotation of the seasons, safeguard its people against stifling within their own agglomeration of stone and brick.

Coat of arms of the Prévôté
(military police establishment)
of the merchants in 1556

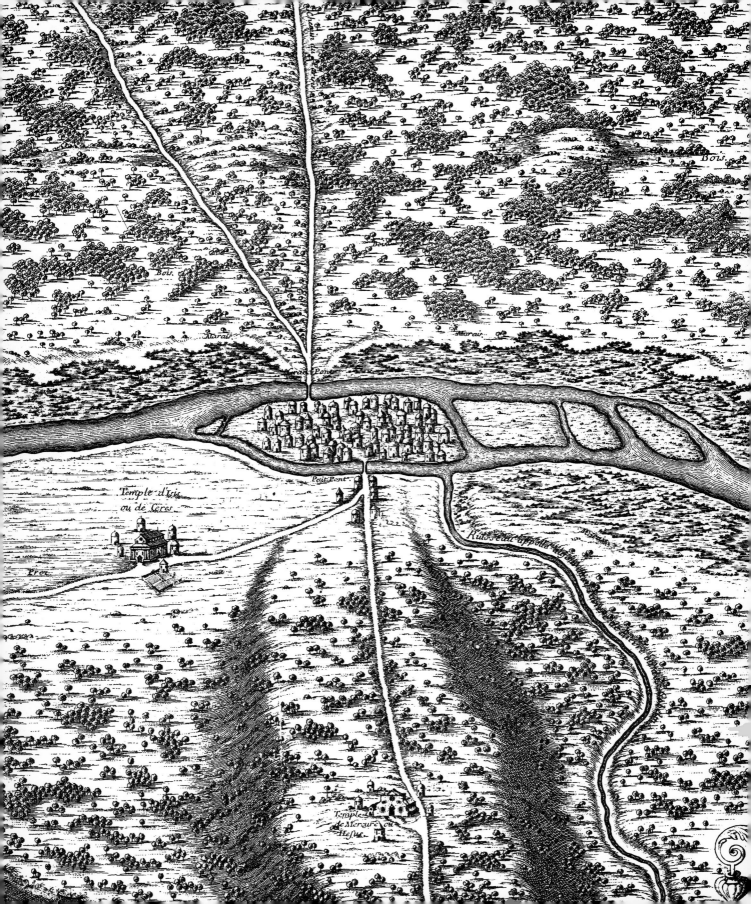

Bois.

Bois.

Marais.

Marais.

Crois Pont.

Petit Pont.

Temple d'Isis
ou de Ceres.

Pret.

Ruisseau appellé

Temple
de Mercure ou
Hesus.

The Cathedral

On that island in the Seine where the *Cité* grew from a maritime trading station at the junction of important routes, where the first sacred buildings, rulers' seats and fortifications of *Lutetia* arose, stands what today is still the most precious edifice of the metropolis: the church of the bishops of Paris. It is from this spot that the distances along the national highways are measured, those arteries which from every point of the compass converge upon the capital. In 1160 Maurice de Sully put in hand the construction of the new cathedral, whose mighty presence overshadows all earlier monuments. Among the marvels of Gothic architecture in northern France, between the splendour of the coronation cathedral of Reims, the mystical richness of Chartres, the soaring vaults of Amiens and the walls of Bourges sparkling with colour, Notre-Dame de Paris proudly stands unparalleled in its solemn dignity. Its very name recalls the sound of deep-throated bells. In the majesty of its noble façade with the squat twin towers surmounting the 'Gallery of Kings', the Gothic vertical style is wedded to the antique horizontal, religious fervour with mathematical precision and artistic imagination.

The carillon of the cathedral leads back by way of Victor Hugo's romantic evocation to the times of Abélard and Héloïse, when the renown of the spiritual school of Paris irradiated the cultural world of its day and the musicians of Notre-Dame contributed towards the triumph of Gothic polyphony. Magnificent processions, sanctifying the nation's life, passed through the richly sculptured portals; but, to a far greater extent, the shrouded interior with its faint shimmer of candles belongs to those who slip in here for quiet communion with God. From time to time revolution surged up to the walls of this holy place: the precious sculptures of the west front were shattered (Viollet-le-Duc subsequently replaced them as exactly as possible), Robespierre here paid homage to the Goddess of Reason, and the *communards* of 1871 murdered the Archbishop. Yet, not even the upheavals of our own times have silenced the bells of Notre-Dame.

The Gallic settlement
Lutetia, after an
eighteenth-century plan

9

The Royal Palace

Just as a man's origins can be made to account for many of his characteristics and talents but never for the uniqueness of his personality, so the familiar face of an incomparable city such as Paris expresses something other, more personal than that which has accrued merely from geographical factors and historical associations. Nevertheless, Paris has been moulded by a sequence of particularly impressive historical events.

Rome became Rome because, from the outset, it was Rome: a city-republic which only the might of the empire it had itself created was ultimately able to crush. London became London because, as the greatest port of a sea-girt land, it developed with the industrial and political growth of the island people. St Petersburg became the hub of a tsardom through an act of will of a ruler. The political significance of Paris, however, derives from a centuries-long, systematic endeavour on the part of the kings of France, whose work was carried on by five republics and two empires. Here, unlike in Rome, centralization was not an established fact from the outset, nor was it the expression of a predetermined unity based on some such principle as 'Blut und Boden' or of a dominion, aimed at cultural development, in the colonial sphere. Rather has it been a secular political process of unification within a racially complex, cultured nation. In contrast to the German Empire of the Middle Ages, which was federal in character because universal in outlook, and with its Emperor peregrinating from one palatinate to another, France developed the organized unified State, the *Etat*. And as the reins of power were gathered within the capital, so the royal palace tended to become the nation's focal building.

The Merovingian monarch Clovis and his successors still resided on the *Cité* island. It was Philip Augustus who before the start of the Crusade (of 1202) had built, as the key point of the fortifications of Paris, a fortress on the spot which at that time already was, for reasons unknown to history, named *le Louvre*; with its mighty central tower, in which both the crown jewels and important prisoners of the State were kept, it had much

Paris in the time
King Philip August
1180–12

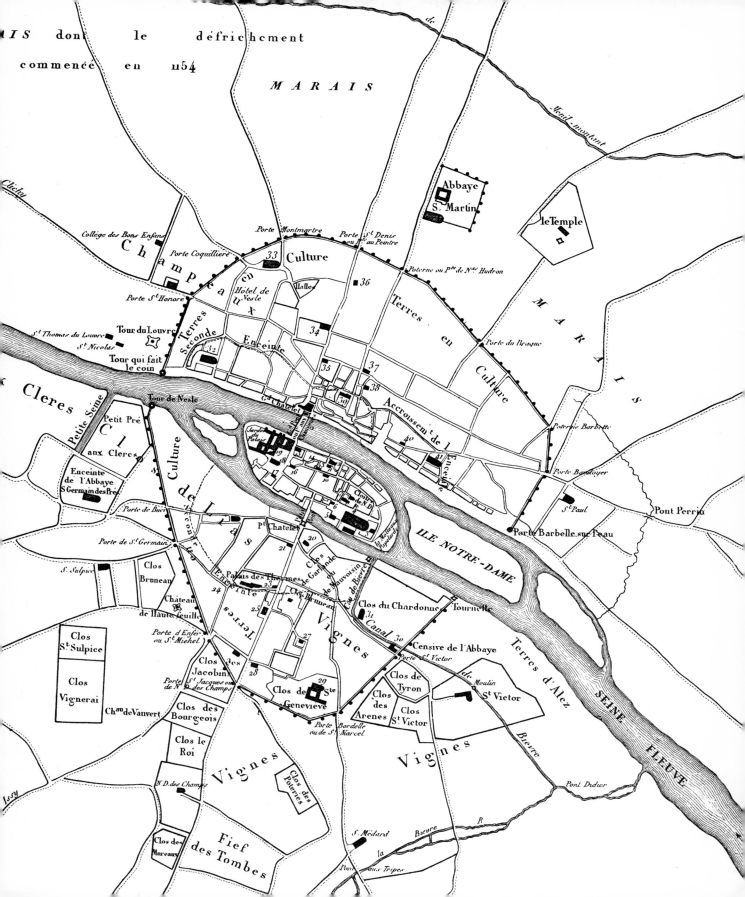

in common with the Tower of London. Its conversion at the time of the Renaissance into a magnificent palace was the work of Francis I, that great friend of the arts; he had the ancient dungeon pulled down and commissioned a new building from Pierre Lescot, which Henry II had erected in slightly modified form and decorated by Jean Goujon – the façade on the left of the clock-tower in the Cour Carrée dates from this period (plates 33, 34). Later rulers were responsible for further extensions: Henry IV – *le bon roi Henri*, who deemed Paris 'well worth a Mass' and who rewarded his people by his tolerant treatment – connected the castle by means of a gallery with Catherine de' Medici's Tuileries, whereby the complex of buildings took on vast proportions.

Louis XIV, who brought the French notion of *l'état* to finality, appointed his great minister Colbert Director of Works for Paris, and charged him with fashioning the royal residence into a superb symbol of sovereignty. The result was the Hôtel and Dôme des Invalides, the Avenue des Champs-Elysées, the Observatory, the Pont Royal, a series of triumphal arches (among them, those of Saint-Denis and Saint-Martin); the city, whose population had meanwhile increased by half a million, became brighter and cleaner. The enlarging of the royal palace was, however, to constitute the climax of this embellishment of the capital. The most renowned architect of the day, the Cavaliere Bernini, was brought over from Rome. The advice of the inspired designer of the colonnade of St Peter's was that all the existing Louvre buildings should be dismantled; in their stead he planned a huge *palazzo* in the Italian Baroque style. But French classicism here, too, gained a victory over the style which held sway over all the neighbouring countries: the standing buildings were to be preserved, the tradition carried on. True, they actually went so far as to hold a ceremony at which the foundation-stone was laid; but, no sooner had the illustrious visitor departed than the Works Commission decided to drop his project altogether. Instead, the plan drawn up by Claude Perrault, I Saint-Germain-des-P staunch believer in the principles of Vitruvius, with its 'Colonnade' forming a characteristic eastern façade, was adopted. Before roof level was II Pont-N

reached the King decided to shake the dust of Paris from his feet, and removed his court to Versailles (1680). Artists thereupon installed themselves in the galleries where they gave themselves over to *la vie bohèmienne*; the Cour Carrée remained a medley of barracks. With difficulty, Marigny, Intendant of Louis XV, saved them from further dilapidation.

It was the Revolution which fetched the King back to his capital: in 1789 Louis XVI moved into the Tuileries, which Napoleon I was later to choose, with rather more freedom of action, as his residence also; this palace, which constituted the western abutment of the whole Louvre complex, remained the seat of supreme power in France until 1870. The Commune of 1871 pillaged the palace, the Third Republic had the ruins demolished; the Pavillon de Flore (plate 38), whence the Empress Eugénie fled into exile, alone remains to testify to the splendid imperial court of Napoleon III.

But a different role had meanwhile been assigned to the Louvre proper. Ever since Francis I had begun to acquire paintings and casts of ancient sculptures, the royal collections had been progressively added to: Louis XIV had embellished his palaces in Paris and Versailles with no less than two thousand paintings. In the eighteenth century Marigny encouraged the founding of a 'museum' in the Grande Galerie; but it was not until 1793 that the Convention realized the ambition of the Enlightenment to make the accumulated art treasures accessible to the general public. Napoleon, who had the Cour Carrée completed and the large North Gallery begun, contributed his share towards making the Louvre as museum even more famous perhaps than it had been as a royal palace. The loss to foreign nations, after the fall of the Emperor, of a part of Napoleon's war booty, was soon more than compensated for by new accessions, purchases and bequests, and by finds which excavations in various parts of the world were increasingly yielding. Under Napoleon III two large pavilions were built adjoining the Squares and the extensive frontage on to the Rue de Rivoli was completed. Both the Third and Fourth Republics safeguarded the Louvre as home of the national collection, thus transferring to the cultural sphere the concept of centralization previously embodied in the royal palace.

Conciergerie

17

Revolution Square

Rome was not built in a day, and the city planning of Paris is far less the product of this or that particular gifted architect than the material expression of an attitude to life which has persisted down the centuries. Thus, the generously conceived sector whose central feature is the Place de la Concorde, with its wide prospects which give the impression of having been planned upon the drawing-board by some bold designer, only gradually acquired its present aspect. It is the spirit of antiquity which here, as also in the landscape gardens of a Le Nôtre, merges with the spirit of the European Enlightenment: the partiality for long, straight avenues, radial effects, studied regularity, precise proportioning and proud display, a feeling for spaciousness which combines a mathematical temperance with worldly elegance – all these here come together to make up the scene of vital historical happenings, where in the place of a monarch a no less imperious actor has since made his bow: the people.

From the neo-Gothic tower in the Place du Louvre one can walk four kilometres virtually in a straight line to the Arc de Triomphe in the Place Charles de Gaulle (formerly the Place de l'Etoile); on the way, one passes through the gateway in Perrault's Louvre façade, the Cour Carrée, the triumphal arch of the Carrousel between the lengthy wings of the New Louvre, the central avenue of the Tuileries gardens, past its ornamental ponds, flower-beds, shrubberies and statues, which still betray the hand of the great Le Nôtre, finally emerging from between the two winged horses of Coysevox into the Concorde – more a landscape than a Square.

At its centre now stands the Obelisk of Rameses II from Luxor, which the Viceroy of Egypt presented to the democratic monarch Louis-Philippe in 1831, replacing the changing symbols of latter-day constitutional forms. On the opposite side the two horse-breakers sculpted by Coustou, on their tall plinths, flank the approach to the Champs-Elysées, which climbs gently up to the mighty Arc de Triomphe well over a mile away. Along this most magnificent avenue in the world, once the scene of parading equipages but

18

now monopolized by speeding automobiles, the imperial cohorts with their flashing emblems and streaming plumes proudly passed; it has borne the regiments of the *poilus*, the armoured columns of the Army of Liberation. Thrice, too, the citizens of Paris have watched with sullen anger, as foreign conquerors usurped this privilege. But on every 14 July the entire nation mobilizes, and excited crowds surge along it amid a sea of tricolour flags.

The Obelisk marks the point where the westward vista intersects the north-south axis; on either side it is flanked by a temple-like arrangement of columns. On the north side alone do the buildings come sufficiently close to produce an effect recalling the disposition of the other Squares. The two palaces erected 1760–75 by Gabriel make up a magnificent frontage, through the centre of which the Rue Royale leads the eye to the Madeleine, monument of purest classicism. To the south the Square is linked with the Left Bank of the Seine by the Concorde Bridge; with its north front dating from the time of the First Empire, the Palais-Bourbon, seat of the National Assembly, constitutes a pendant to the Madeleine.

During the first half of the eighteenth century what is now the Place de la Concorde was an untended esplanade at the city's fringe, where blocks of marble for the buildings and sculptures lay haphazardly. By 1757 work was being started on a conversion planned by Gabriel, which turned it into an octagonal laid-out area bounded by fosses, with pavilions, lawns and statues. The year 1762 saw the erection there of Bouchardon's equestrian statue of Louis XV, 'Le Bien Aimé', from whence the *Place* derived its name. When, eight years later, his successor married Marie-Antoinette, destiny cast a dark shadow upon the couple: in the mêlée attendant upon the celebration fireworks 133 spectators were hurled into the fosses and killed. As in 1792 the Revolution mounted towards its climax, the Square was rechristened 'Place de la Revolution', and the royal effigy disappeared. On 21 January 1793 the guillotine was erected here for the first time, and the executioner Sanson held up the head of Louis XVI for the jeering crowds to see. On 11 May the instrument of death went into action once again – but it was erected not, as in the first place, on the

The Old T
between Notre-D
the Tuileries and the a
of Saint-Germain-des-
after the plan of Vassa
known as Nicolay,

20

Champs-Elysées side, but over towards the Tuileries – and now heads rolled in an ever more furious tempo: Marie-Antoinette, Philippe Egalité, Danton and well over a thousand others mounted the scaffold. By 1794 it was Robespierre's own turn, soon after which the bloody drama drew to its close.

The Directory gave the place of execution its reconciliatory new name, 'Place de la Concorde'. Three times more the Square was renamed: the Bourbons, returning to power in 1814, called it 'Place Louis XV' again, which was changed to 'Place Louis XVI' in 1823; the Revolution of 1830 reverted to the name 'Place de la Concorde'. Under Louis-Philippe two fountains were added to the Obelisk in imitation of St Peter's Square, while Gabriel's eight pavilions were made to serve as bases for female statues symbolizing France's cities – among them that of Strasbourg, before which the patriotic demonstrators gathered after 1871. Napoleon III had the fosses filled in, thereby lending the Square its present aspect. This century has seen mechanized transport take possession of the broad areas, and its tempo invests the place with a new, dynamic life. But, over and above this, the Concorde – which now finds itself in the centre instead of on the periphery of this city of mounting millions – continues to serve as the stage for solemn processions and vast concourses. At any time, though, the people of France – true to the traditions of the Great Revolution – may foregather here for the purpose of dictating the law of history to the gentlemen in the Palais-Bourbon close by.

Ward seal from the time of the Great Revolution

The Stage of Europe

'All roads lead to Rome'; but it is to the *Ville Lumière* that men and women of culture have for long felt themselves drawn as by a magnet. Paris has been the arbiter not only of women's fashions, but of furnishing, cuisine, painting, literature and politics, leading the taste of the Western world where these things are concerned. This trend reached its peak in the nineteenth century, despite the unrest which, since the French Revolution, has hounded one Administration after the other out of office. Not only has this political instability failed to lessen the city's prestige, it has even tended to lend Paris an additional kaleidoscopic fascination.

The enigmatic person of the Prince-President and Second Emperor, with his comfortable paunch and provocative 'imperial', symbolizes an epoch whose brilliance recalls the Periclean Age: Victor Hugo, Musset, Balzac, Flaubert, Renan, Zola and Baudelaire were producing incomparable works of poetry and prose; the composers Cherubini, Berlioz, Rossini, the great masters of the Opéra-Comique down to Bizet and Offenbach were adding to the world's repertoire of music; Delacroix, Corot, Courbet, Daumier and Manet were infusing fresh life into painting, Pasteur was making his vital discoveries in the field of medicine. Richard Wagner and the young Verdi, too, following in the footsteps of Gluck, were seeking in the French capital the highest laurels the world has to offer. Even so, we have mentioned only the more illustrious names; Paris had become the arena for an unprecedented display of talents, indeed of genius – and of vanity. Baron Haussmann, under imperial warrant, carved wide boulevards through the huddle of houses, while technical science introduced such amenities as drainage, street lighting and new methods of transport and communication. The two Great Exhibitions of 1855 and 1867 became the world's rendezvous, and this many-sided city gained a new industry – the business of amusing its manifold visitors. Not more than seven years after the Prussians in their spiked helmets had marched across the Concorde and the fury of the revolutionary elements within the Commune had once again subsided, yet another Great Exhibition was staged – in place of the Emperor, the dapper Presidents of the Third Republic now presiding – and the World Exhibition of 1889 gave Paris its new emblem, the Eiffel Tower, symbol of a new era. The French capital, which in the light of the 'follow-my-leader' activities of the Administration and Montmartre's addiction to light-hearted amusement had come to be regarded by foreign observers as sunk in helpless depravity, rose up again in all its vigour following the hardships of the First World War. Even though we may smile a little sceptically at the contention of earnest Parisians that in France's capital alone do people properly understand how to paint, write poetry, act, eat, make love and dress, we are ready to admit that it is virtually impossible to imagine a viable European culture without Paris – today, no less than in former times.

In the summer of 1945 the wonder-city presented a shocking spectacle, even though, as if by a miracle – in which certain courageous individuals in both the home and the enemy camp had a hand – it had been spared any major war-damage. The streets swarming with foreign soldiery, the stinking *Métro* trains, the profiteers' dens, the barren, crumbling house-fronts all betokened a state of corruption which seemed to offer no hope of genuine recovery. But within a few years Paris once again – and this time more convincingly perhaps than ever before – gave the lie to the legend of degeneration. To the customary accompaniment of ministerial crises the giant city has got back into its stride, has recaptured the industry, the vitality, the elegance and the brightness with which we are wont to associate it.

Barriere de Pantin.

iv Dôme des Invali‹
v Quai de Monteb‹

24

From Fortress to Agglomeration

Since 1954, when the first English edition of this book appeared, Paris too has seen the years of improvisation and makeshift organization over which the two World Wars cast their shadow give way to an era of consolidation and far-sighted planning. Guarded as a fortress until the outbreak of the Second World War, Paris has been facing the consequences of having become an agglomeration reaching far out into the surrounding countryside.

At the end of 1958, a man aspired to the Elysée Palace who created a new Republic – the Fifth – in his own image and who for a decade combined in his person the power and authority of the centralized State in the manner of the former kings of France and the two Napoleons. And even if the city no longer radiates that omnipresent *grandeur* of former days, yet the *Ville Lumière* has lost little of its lustre and its power to attract. Despite the impersonal international character of the many-storeyed blocks that are springing up in increasing numbers round the old town core, the city on the Seine remains as ever the expression of all the dynamism and manifold talents of a truly great nation.

It befits the imperial style of the de Gaulle era, that during it clear-cut directions, long overdue, for the development of Paris were issued, just as had been done by Colbert at the behest of Louis XIV and by Haussmann for Napoleon III. The problem to be solved was formulated by the historian Marcel Poète in 1929: 'Advances in scientific knowledge have caused Paris to expand immeasurably. We must see to it that the same advances shall now, by applying them to transportation, serve to restore to the city more freedom to breathe. One has only to create several satellite towns, sufficiently removed from Paris and not directly outside its gates (as was done in the case of the projected housing estate in La Courneuve), on rural territory, and after the establishment of traffic routes and the necessary urban installations prior to the handing over of building land. Between these satellite towns and Paris a natural play of forces should

Canal Saint-Martin

29

develop, in order to bring the demands of urban living into a state of equilibrium.'*

The law of 2 August 1961 created the District de la Région de Paris, and three years later there followed as a further step the abolition of the former *départements* of Seine and Seine-et-Oise, and the subdivision of the region into the eight *départements*: Paris (*intra muros*), Seine-et-Marne, Yvelines, Essonne, Hauts-de-Seine, Seine-Saint-Denis, Val-de-Marne and Val-d'Oise. In June 1965, the *Schéma directeur d'aménagement et d'urbanisme de la Région de Paris* was finally published, pointing the way to the next ten years of development. The aim of all these moves was to 'transform' the vast concentration of people at the centre of the Paris basin 'into a better adjusted and more human urban community' (*l'agglomération se transformant en une région urbaine mieux equilibre et plus humaine*).

Seventy per cent of the landscape of the Ile-de-France, in which Paris lies embedded, consists of fertile arable land, while a further 20 per cent is covered with trees and shrubs. Here lie the fifteen smaller townships and a thousand rural communities whose fate, in the face of the capital's invasion of their territory, must no longer be left to chance, above all within the area of agglomeration of 1,200 sq. km. with its all but 10 million inhabitants. Further expansion is seen in terms of an effective division into residential and industrial zones, and the early completion of the road and rail links in the context of eight satellite towns of 300,000 to 800,000 inhabitants apiece round the old town core.

The demographic development is already moving in the intended direction. The influx from the provinces into the capital is no longer uncontrollable: between 1962 and 1968, the agglomeration increased by 1,100,000 inhabitants, whereas the population of the city itself dropped by 200,000 during the same period. Half of the total increase resulted from the surplus of births, the other half can be attributed in equal proportions to immigrants from the provinces and from abroad. Other centres, like

* Quoted from a lecture delivered by Paul Delouvrier, Délégué général au District de la Région de Paris, on 6 February 1966 before an audience of councillors and magistrates.

Montpellier, Grenoble, Toulouse, Toulon, as well as Lyon and Marseille, show a greater percentage increase, and the contribution of Greater Paris to France's over-all population dropped from 29 per cent in 1954 to 26 per cent in 1968.

This book, it is true, does not contain photographs of any parts of the city that extend beyond its old defensive and customs frontiers, nor will those who take up this book devoted to Paris expect to find them between its covers. The inclusion of such historical localities contained within the present-day District of Paris as Saint-Denis, Versailles, Malmaison, Saint-Germain-en-Laye, Chantilly, Fontainebleau, Melun, Meaux, would call for several volumes of this nature. As for the new complexes that are mushrooming up, it is as yet impossible to tell to what extent the massive blocks of concrete and steel and glass, the bridges, fly-overs and underpasses, built in the International Style of the second half of the twentieth century, will be distinguishable from similar constructions anywhere else on this planet. For these reasons we are limiting ourselves to the Paris that irresistibly draws visitors from all over the world, that historic polygon which with its 25 sq. km. makes up only a quarter of the modern city of Paris and a fiftieth of the agglomeration of Greater Paris; the essential Paris, where churches and palaces abound, with the façades of its buildings newly cleaned and gleaming – for which the Minister of Culture André Malraux was responsible – and with its countless sites that recall notable historical and cultural events.

Barriere de Fontainebleau (9)

Villages and Towns

France has paid a high price for the prestige of a capital which is the Athens of our time. In the Middle Ages the French towns with their proud cathedrals and abbeys were still vying with one another for the honour of exalting a culture dedicated to the greater glory of Christ; today everything that lives outside the confines of Paris has sunk to the level of mere provincialism. The seat of Government, the High Court of Jurisdiction, the National Museums, the Finance and War Ministries, the leading schools and finest theatres, the most important research centres – everything, in fact, fell to the lot of Paris. And, even if André George in his introduction to the admirable *Guide Bleu* to Paris offers the provinces the consolation that at least the capital does not aspire to the renown of regional cooking, nevertheless the best cooks and finest vintages from France's famous vineyards nearly always manage to find their way to Paris. What is more, those who earn their money in other parts of the country, spend it as far as possible in the metropolis.

Such a concentration of material and intellectual resources was bound to exercise its attraction far beyond the frontiers of France, particularly as an easy tolerance, at least towards artists and the black-coated fraternity, has been preserved as an inalienable right throughout all the changes in the Constitution. Contributing to the city's renown are guests from all manner of sovereign States, among them emigrants, exiles, confirmed bohemians, and, above all, artists, who have settled on the banks of the Seine because nowhere else could they find the desired climate.

Centralization is clearly recognizable in this concentration of people and their buildings: in the large Squares and Avenues, the long rows of houses, the ornamental façades of public buildings, in the statues of crowned goddesses, in the ceremonies of the tricolour standard-bearers and the *camions* of the Police, ever on the alert. But this is only one facet of Paris. In contrast to the centralization of the State we have the characteristic individualism of the citizens. Paris, where impersonal officialdom

VII Pont Alexan

is so widespread, is at the same time the most human of cities. The real life of the community is played out in the sphere of everyday experience, as we see it manifested in the market, the school and the church, in the workshop and the local café. In the separate districts the *genius loci* of the former country parishes and of the manors, villages and towns which grew up round the abbeys, still holds sway. There, rising up to north and south of the Seine, lie Montparnasse and Montmartre, facing one another. Upon the Ile Saint-Louis a quiet, aristocratic little eighteenth-century town survives; in the Marais, on the other hand, about the Place des Vosges, the once elegant milieu has yielded to a lower-middle-class one. In the Place du Tertre in old Montmartre one feels oneself back in Murger's *Bohème* of one hundred years ago. About the venerable abbey church of Saint-Germain-des-Prés, the cafés are filled with young people engaged in heated argument over the issues of the day; near by, the narrow streets round the Carrefour de Buci, with their abundance of vegetables and fruit, happy hunting-ground of housewives, at times resemble Oriental bazaars. In the Latin Quarter about the Panthéon, students of every nationality continue to throng the pavements even since the splendid Cité Universitaire by the Porte d'Arcueil was built. To the west, beyond the Champs-Elysées, stand the palaces of the old and the new aristocracies, whose fortunes managed to survive – or owe their origin to – inflation and bankruptcy.

The *faubourgs* have long since become integral parts of Paris proper, while farther out, a ring of new proletarian suburbs with factories, warehouses and stadia have grown up. Amid the jostling crowds on the *Métro* trains and omnibuses, amid the lures of the city's purchasable wares, the glitter of expensive restaurants, the collective truculence of officialdom, we come face to face on every side with rustic idylls, evidences of an easygoing provincial way of life and the obliging graces of individual men and women. Parks and courtyards serve as playgrounds for the children: there they yell with delight at the antics of Punch and Judy, or mount the tireless painted horses of the roundabouts; across the ornamental ponds of the

Tuileries the toy boats sail their races. Nursemaids, elderly gentlemen with grey gloves, a youth deep in a book, and lovers – many pairs of lovers – sit upon shaded benches, their thoughts far away. Along the banks of the Seine beneath the *Quais* and the bridges over which the traffic roars, the tramp settles himself for a nap, his half-emptied bottle of red wine beside him, while peaceful anglers sit waiting patiently for a bite.

And yet we have still not captured the distinctive charm of Paris, that aura which encompasses all that is contrasted, significant and trivial. Is it due to the light which falls upon each façade, caressing alike the cold splendour of palaces and prosaic faces of business houses old and new? Or does it, perhaps, result from the prevailing silver-grey, the richest, subtlest, most ethereal of all colours, the colour of France's greatest painters?

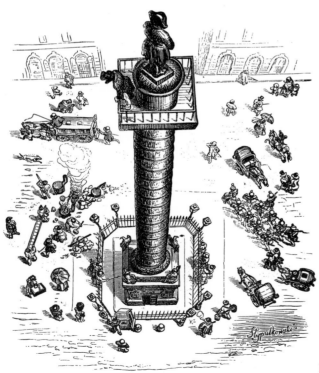

Place Vendôme

The City as Monument

From among the many aspects of Paris which could be presented and extolled, we have, in the sequence of pictures that follow, chosen the 'monumental'; for ours is objective reporting rather than the impressionist interpretation which is the prerogative of a Utrillo, a Vivin, a Dufy or a Matisse. We try to show what, amid the perpetual flux, is enduring; the monument in stone which the city itself has erected, which is at the same time a monument to the cultivated mind. And so its more permanent features predominate; our pictures concentrate more upon the vessel than its content, depict the buildings rather than the life of the people which will always reflect the changing moods of the nation.

In the Middle Ages all the spiritual, intellectual and artistic energies of the period contributed towards the building of a church, which became therefore the universal monument of an epoch. Latterly the architect has become the servant of a temporal overlord, his works have had to express the power of the State and satisfy the tastes of people in high positions. Even an ecclesiastical building such as the Dôme des Invalides proclaims the glory of the Sun King rather than the glory of God, while the Madeleine and the Panthéon serve as well as halls of honour as they do as places of worship. The architect has been reduced to the level of other creative artists; a bureau by the cabinet-maker Cressent is almost as true an expression of his time as a façade by the architect Gabriel. If the palm is to be awarded to any one section of those who further the interests of culture, it must go to the Men of Letters whose academy is to be found beneath the cupola of the Institut de France.

Though architectural design has been guided by the orderly hand of reason, it has remained the regal expression of the spirit of France. Rightly, the Colonnade of the learned Perrault was given preference over the great Bernini's project, while the reinforced concrete constructions of Perret are more in keeping with the place than the inventions of a Le Corbusier, inspired though they are in their own specialized way. Everything serves communal ends, is designed to fall in with the humanist tradition of antiquity: parallel lines, symmetry, carefully worked-out proportions, clarity of conception, spaciousness, a preference for what is logical, a desire to do things on a large scale while avoiding unwieldiness. Our aim, then, is to show the buildings of Paris as monuments to the cultivated mind; a worthy contribution on the part of the French genius to the works of man.

IX Rue Chap

Notre-Dame and the Medieval City

1–4 NOTRE-DAME, the cathedral church of the Archbishop of Paris, is situated on the Ile de la Cité. A temple was probably standing on the same spot as long ago as the first century. The earliest church – believed to be of the fourth century – was dedicated to St Stephen; it was next to this that the first church of Notre-Dame arose in the sixth century. During the twelfth century, as a result of the movement which produced the mighty Gothic cathedrals in the north of France, it was decided to erect a new church on the site of the two earlier ones. Soon after his enthronement in 1160 Bishop Maurice de Sully began building, and by 1330 most of the work had been completed.

1 The cathedral seen from the Quai de Montebello on the opposite bank of the Seine, providing an unimpeded view of the bold flying buttresses of the apse. The slender spire above the crossing, 90 m. high, overtops the characteristic west towers by 21 m.; it is a replica of the thirteenth-century spire destroyed at the end of the eighteenth century, and was built 1859/60 by the renowned architect and restorer Viollet-le-Duc.

2 View of the cathedral from the Quai Saint-Michel, past the south-east corner of the Palais de Justice. This aspect shows the magnificent west front with its three porches completed in 1208, the 'Gallery of Kings' and its statues of the forbears of Christ (destroyed, like the majority of large-scale images, during the Revolution and later replaced); above this, the storey containing the great rose window of 1220–25, the fretted gallery and the twin towers completed in 1250.

3 The tympanum of the right-hand, oldest porch of the west front, the 'Porch of Saint Anne', contains a statue of the Virgin enthroned holding the Child, whose hand is raised in blessing. It dates from 1165–70.

4 The south transept, renovated 1258, with its grand rose window.

5, 6 The QUAI DE MONTEBELLO (see also colour plate V). On the Seine embankments the *bouquinistes* have, ever since the previous century, offered their wares for sale; besides antiquarian books of all sorts, these comprise old and new prints, postcards and postage stamps.

7 In the old quarter on the left bank opposite Notre-Dame, on the site previously occupied by the priory where the sixth-century chronicler Gregory of Tours lived, now stands the venerable little church of SAINT-JULIEN-LE-PAUVRE, the oldest in Paris.

8 The HÔTEL DE SENS was built 1474–1519 in the Gothic style by the Spanish-born Archbishop Tristan de Salazar, as archiepiscopal see for Sens, to which the bishopric of Paris was subordinate until its elevation to an archbishopric in 1623. From 1605 to 1615, after her separation from Henry IV, Margaret of Valois held court here, and Gabriele d'Annunzio occupied the palace in 1911 while writing his *Martyre de saint*

Sebastien, later set to music by Debussy. Since 1912 the building has been owned by the city and today houses the Forney Library.

9 On the Ile de la Cité, above the entrance to the Palais de Justice with its splendid wrought-iron gates by Bigonnet (1783–85), rises LA SAINTE-CHAPELLE, a gem of the Gothic period at its height (1246–48). It was built by Saint Louis of France to receive Christ's Crown of Thorns and other relics.

10 View from the Quai de Conti across the Seine, showing the northern part of the PONT-NEUF where it approaches the western tip of the Ile de la Cité, and the two stone and brick buildings from the time of Louis XIII that border the Place Dauphine on the west. (See also colour plate II, showing the southern end of the Pont-Neuf and the equestrian statue of Henry IV of 1818 by which the former statue of 1614, destroyed in 1792, was replaced.)

Colour plate III (page 16). The PONT AU CHANGE, the bridge connecting the right bank of the Seine with the Ile de la Cité (so called since the twelfth century), was built in its present form in 1858. Beyond is the CONCIERGERIE, characterized by its fourteenth-century bastion-like towers, the Tour César and the Tour d'Argent, and part of the complex of buildings constituting the Palais de Justice, on the Quai de l'Horloge. At the time of the Revolution prominent prisoners were kept in the Conciergerie prior to being taken to the guillotine. The tower at the near corner of the building is the Tour de l'Horloge (clock-tower) dating from the reign of Philip IV 'le Bel', and frequently rebuilt since.

City seal of 1577

2

3

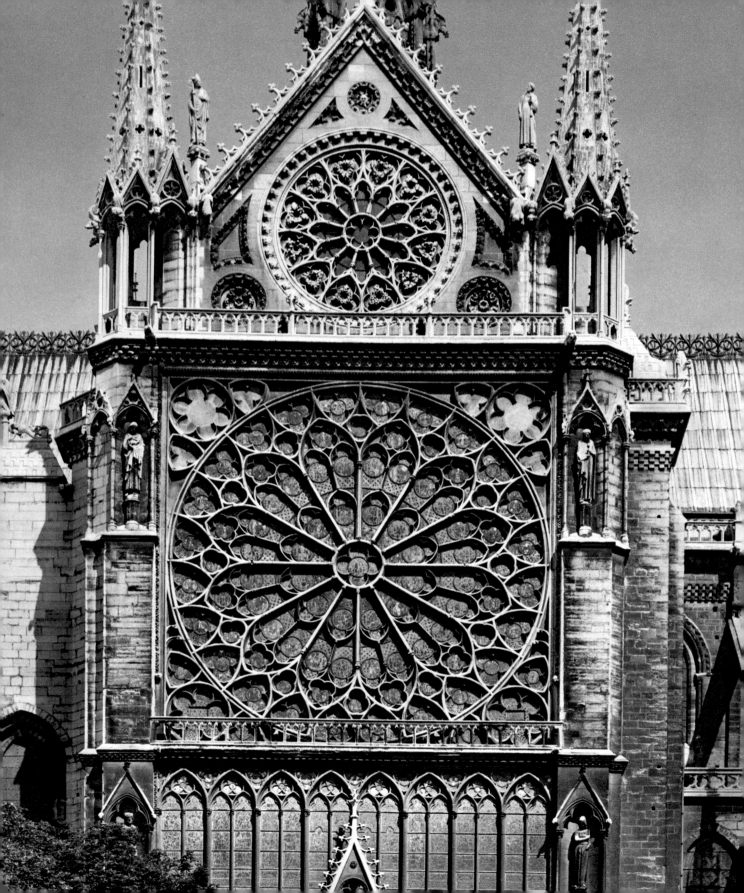

6

5, 6 QUAI DE MONTEBELLO

7

8

10 PONT-NEUF

Old Paris around the Seine Islands

11 PONT MARIE links the Ile Saint-Louis with the right bank of the Seine. This bridge, built 1618–35, is named after Monsieur Marie, the 'Entrepreneur général des ports de France', who, in 1614, joined the two islands 'aux Vache' and 'Notre-Dame' into the present Ile Saint-Louis.

12 The Gothic TOUR SAINT-JACQUES, dating from 1508–22, is the only part of the church of Saint-Jacques-la-Boucherie by the Châtelet, founded in Carolingian times, to survive demolition in 1797.

13 The basilica of SACRÉ-CŒUR (77) set on the hill of Montmartre dominates the sky-line in this view from the towers of Notre-Dame; in the foreground, right, the Tour Saint-Jacques (12) and, left, the church of Saint-Eustache (17).

14 The HÔTEL DE VILLE, which houses the city authorities, was built in 1882 by Ballu and Deperthes in a style that has affinities with that of the Renaissance building that originally stood here but was destroyed during the Communard rising of 1871. The elaborate façades are embellished with 136 statues of famous people.

15 In 1862 the present Pont Louis-Philippe replaced a suspension-bridge built in 1833 during the reign of the 'bourgeois king' Louis-Philippe. Beyond can be seen the terraced houses of the Ile Saint-Louis and of the Ile de la Cité which the Pont Saint-Louis connects with the former.

16 The QUAI DE BOURBON on the Ile Saint-Louis, where a corner of the old, aristocratic Paris is preserved almost intact. Nearly every one of the seventeenth- and eighteenth-century private mansions has a plaque commemorating some famous resident.

17 The church of SAINT-EUSTACHE, in the quarter of the now-disused covered markets (Les Halles), was built 1532–1637 to plans by Pierre Lemercier. The structure of the church is Gothic, with rich ornamentation in the Renaissance manner. One of the most important centres for the promotion of Church music, it witnessed the

burial of Rameau, the funeral service for Mozart's mother, and first performances of works by Berlioz, Liszt and others.

18, 19 The elaborate façade of the Late Gothic church of SAINT-GERVAIS-SAINT-PROTAIS with its Ionic and Corinthian pillars dates from 1616–21 and was designed by Clément Métezeau, Louis XIII in person having laid the first stone. Of the organists who played the seventeenth-century organ, no less than eight were members of the famous Couperin family of musicians, and Nicolas, Armand-Louis and Pierre-Louis Couperin are among the distinguished persons laid to rest in the church.

During the Revolution the church was temporarily converted into a 'Temple of Youth'. On Good Friday, 29 March 1918, a German shell pierced the ceiling of the church, killing fifty-one people.

The old Hôtel de Ville, after an engraving of 1778

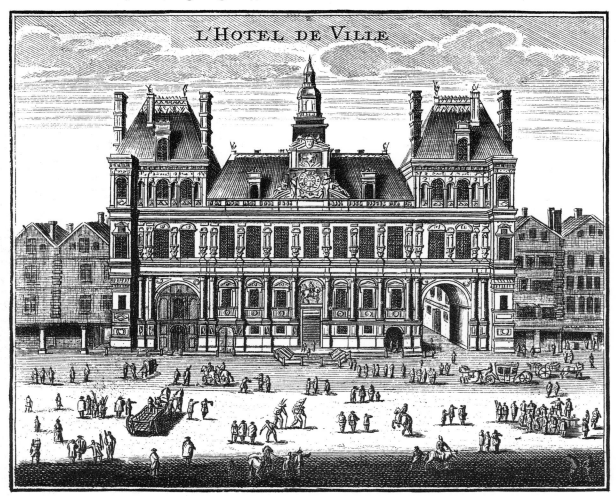

12 TOUR SAINT-JACQUES

13 TOUR SAINT-JACQU
ST-EUSTACHE,
MONTMARTRE

14 HÔTEL DE VILLE

15
PONT
LOUIS-PHILIPPE

18, 19 SAINT-GERVAIS-SAINT-PROTAIS

In the Old Quarters of the Eastern Districts

20 The HÔTEL DE SOUBISE, with its magnificent courtyard built by the architect Delamair (1705–09), is one of the distinguished private mansions which arose in the sixteenth–seventeenth centuries in the Quartier des Marais. Since 1808 the Archives de France have been kept there.

21 The HÔTEL DE LA VRILLIÈRE, built 1635–38 by François Mansart, was converted by Robert de Cotte for the Comte Toulouse in 1713–19. Since 1811 it has housed the Banque de France, founded in 1800. Today the Administration meets in the GALERIE DORÉE which is over 50 m. long and contains Vassé's statues in gilded wood.

22 The HÔTEL CARNAVALET, in the Marais, was built in 1548 for the head of parliament, de Lignèris. After him it was inhabited by the widow of de Kernevenoy, of which 'Carnavalet' is a corruption. It was enlarged 1655–61 by François Mansart and between 1677 and 1696 was occupied by Madame de Sévigné, whose letters are famous in literature. In 1866 the Palais was bought by the city of Paris and made into the city's Historical Museum in 1880. Our picture shows the view into the Renaissance courtyard with Coysevox's bronze statue of Louis XIV (1689), and the Corps de logis; the reliefs on the wall were probably executed in the workshops of Goujon.

23 Among the many fine Squares in Paris, the PLACE DES VOSGES is the oldest and perhaps also the most attractive. It was built by Henry IV in 1605 with the specific instructions that a large rectangular open space was to be set aside to 'give the inhabitants, badly crowded in their houses', the opportunity to walk about, and further, that the surrounding houses were to show 'an even symmetry, as an ornament to the town'. The ensemble of Renaissance façades, with their attractive combination of white hewn stone and red brick, is still almost completely intact. In the seventeenth century, as the 'Place Royale', the Square was a meeting-place for the fashionable world of the day; in 1799 it was given its present name in honour of the *département* which had been the first to pay its taxes.

24 The ARÈNES DE LUTÈCE is the name given to the area where the Romans constructed a theatre complex in the second or third century AD on the slope of the Sainte-Geneviève heights and which has been excavated and restored since 1869.

25 The grounds of the JARDIN DES PLANTES, an area covering some 70 acres, were planned by Henry IV and Sully in connection with the Botanical Gardens of Montpellier; they became a reality in 1626 during the reign of Louis XIII through the activities of the doctors Jean Hérouard and Guy de la Brosse, the Gardens' first superintendents. Ever since, the Gardens, together with their associated Institutes, have been the scene of operations of many natural scientists of note, and became world-famous above all through Buffon, who filled the office of Superintendent from 1739 to 1788. Carlus's statue of Buffon stands at the end of the long stretch of gardens that leads from the main entrance to the Zoological Museum.

26 The entrance gateway to the extensive buildings and grounds of the HÔPITAL SAINT-LOUIS. The hospital was built 1607–12 by Villefaux at the behest of Henry IV to house victims of the plague; at that time it stood in what were still entirely rural surroundings outside the Porte Saint-Martin.

27 For the first $4\frac{1}{2}$ km. of its length the CANAL SAINT-MARTIN, constructed in the nineteenth century, passes through the former eastern suburbs on the right bank of the Seine, and with the aid of nine largely underground locks facilitates the passage of freight-barges between the Bassin de la Villette and the Seine. (See also colour plate VI showing a barge in the lock which gives access to the tunnel leading under the Boulevards Jules-Ferry and Richard-Lenoir and the Place de la Bastille to the Port de l'Arsenal.)

28 The PLACE DE LA BASTILLE where on 14 July 1789 the prison of the Bastille (already more or less ineffectual by that time) was stormed, and which remained a centre of revolutionary activity even after the demolition (1790) of this symbolical fortress. Since 1841 the July Column, a monument by Alavoine and Duc to the July Rising of 1803, has stood here.

LA BASTILLE

Engraving of 1778

23 PLACE
DES VOSGES

24

25

26

27

28 PLACE DE LA BASTILLE

The Louvre

29 The 'COLONNADE', which forms the eastern abutment of the Louvre (see Introduction), is based on a design jointly drawn up by a commission formed by Colbert, and composed of Le Vau, Lebrun and Claude Perrault. The design was later amplified by Perrault to allow for the extension of the royal apartments.

30 The south façade of the Louvre, shown here, forms one side of the magnificent Cour Carrée, which is bounded on the remaining sides by the other three wings. Begun by Lemercier, work on it was continued after 1660 by Le Vau, its third storey being added in the time of Napoleon by Percier and Fontaine.

31 Buildings opposite the eastern façade of the Louvre, on the PLACE DU LOUVRE: the neo-Gothic tower and carillon built by Ballu in 1860; on the right, Saint-Germain-l'Auxerrois, the church of the Royal Palace, begun in the twelfth century, with a fifteenth-century façade in the *style flamboyant*; on the left, the Mairie des 1er arrondissements, built in 1859 by Hittorf as a pendant to the church.

32 The PALAIS DE L'INSTITUT DE FRANCE stands on the left bank of the Seine, opposite the Louvre. It is capped by the famous 'coupole', beneath which gather the 'Immortals' of the French Academy, founded by Richelieu in 1635. As well as being the home of the Académie française, the Institut houses the Académies des Inscriptions et Belles-Lettres, Sciences, Beaux-Arts and des Sciences morales et politiques. The building, which had its present functions assigned to it by Napoleon in 1805, derives from a foundation by Cardinal Mazarin. It was designed by Louis Le Vau.

33, 34 The east façade of the Louvre fronting on to the COUR CARRÉE, to the left of the clock-tower, is one of the masterpieces of French Renaissance architecture. It was begun in the reign of Francis I and completed in that of Henry II. The architect was Pierre Lescaut, the sculptural decoration being executed by Jean Goujon and his workshop. The relief panel in the centre of the top storey (33) depicts the symbols of war, with Mars, Bellone, and two prisoners, and, in the pediment itself, two deities of victory and the King's initial.

35 The east façade of the east wing of the Cour Carrée, with the PAVILLON SULLY backing on to the clock-tower. Designed by Lescot and Lemercier, it was a mid-nineteenth-century addition to the two large side wings of the Square with its open west end.

36 The GRANDE GALERIE or Galerie du Bord de l'eau in the south wing of the Louvre, begun under Charles IX and completed under Louis XIV. Restoration work carried out in the nineteenth century considerably changed the appearance of the interior. The masterpieces displayed in the great gallery (274 m. long and 10 m. wide) are mostly by painters of the Italian Renaissance.

37 The ARC DE TRIOMPHE DU CARROUSEL in the centre of the Square between the Louvre and the Tuileries, while in the Empire style, is modelled on the triumphal arch of Septimius Severus in Rome. It was erected 1806–08 by Denon to the designs of Percier and Fontaine. The reliefs, by various artists, glorify the victories of Napoleon. The bronze quadriga at the top, representing Peace Triumphant, was added by Bosio in 1828 in celebration of the Restoration.

38 The PONT ROYAL, built 1685–89 by P. Romain, the Dominican, and J. Gabriel, to Mansart's designs. The PAVILLON DE FLORE, at the western end of the Grande Galerie du Louvre, stands on its north side. Once part of the Palace of the Tuileries, it was renovated during the Second Empire by Lefuel.

The Louvre and the Tuileries on Merian's plan of 1615

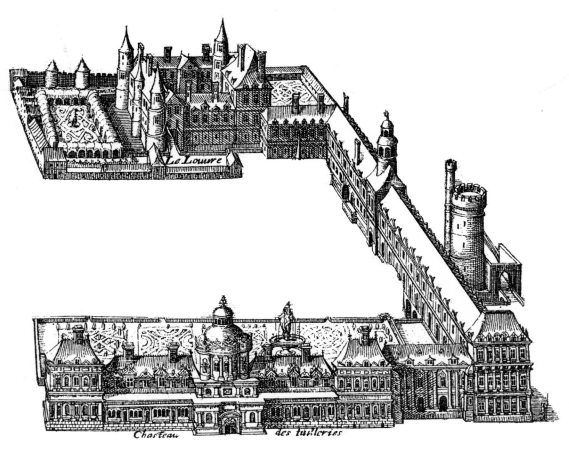

29 LOUVRE

34

35

36

38 PONT ROYAL, PAVILLON DE FLORE

Place de la Concorde · Place Charles de Gaulle

39 The PLACE DE LA CONCORDE was laid out in 1755, when it was named the Place Louis XV. In 1836 Bouchardon's equestrian statue of Louis XV, which had stood in the centre of the Square from 1763 to 1792, was replaced by the Obelisk presented to King Louis-Philippe by Mehemet Ali, Viceroy of Egypt. Its transportation and erection were celebrated as a major event.

The approach to the Champs-Elysées, which forms the westward extension to the Place Charles de Gaulle of the east-west axis running eastwards through the Tuileries Gardens and across the Place du Caroussel as far as the Cour Carrée of the Louvre, has been flanked since 1795 by two statues of horse-breakers (the right-hand group is here illustrated) by Guillaume Coustou. These formerly stood in the grounds of the palace at Marly; hence their name of LES CHEVAUX DE MARLY.

40, 41 At the entrance to the Tuileries Gardens, opposite the Champs-Elysées, stand the two winged horses by Antoine Coysevox which were brought here in 1719 from the palace at Marly. 40 The figure of LA RENOMMÉE, with the Place de la Concorde behind and, right, the Hôtel Crillon. 41 The figure of MERCURY, with the Eiffel Tower beyond.

42, 43 The Obelisk at the centre of the Place de la Concorde is flanked on the north and south sides by the two fountains designed by Hittorf and erected 1836–46. Beyond can be seen the monumental northern periphery of the Square, where the Rue Royale leads between the HÔTEL CRILLON (left) and the Admiralty, both built 1760–75 by Gabriel, to the MADELEINE (47), which has its counterpart, the Palais-Bourbon (46), at the other end of the north–south axis.

44 At the western end of the Champs-Elysées, in the centre of the Place Charles de Gaulle (as the Place de l'Etoile is now named in memory of France's great soldier-President), stands the ARC DE TRIOMPHE (50 m. high) which Napoleon built in honour of his armies. Chalgrin produced the plans in 1806, but work progressed slowly, stopped altogether during the Restoration, and was not completed until 1832–36, in the reign of Louis-Philippe. In 1840 a solemn procession carrying Napoleon's bier passed under the arch on its way to Paris, an honour which was also accorded the poet Victor Hugo in 1885. Certain events, particularly the ceremonial burial of an unknown soldier held beneath its arch on 11 November 1920, and the victory parades of 1919 and 1945 have made the Arc de Triomphe into a national memorial.

45 The most famous of the four large reliefs which adorn the Arc de Triomphe in the Place Charles de Gaulle is on the right of the arch as approached from the Champs-Elysées. Popularly known as 'La Marseillaise', it depicts 'The Volunteers' Departure in 1792' and is considered to be the finest of the works of the sculptor François Rude (1836).

46 The PALAIS-BOURBON, whose characteristic north front faces the Pont de la Concorde and the Place de la Concorde while the south entrance opens on to the Place du Palais-Bourbon, was built 1722–28 for the Duchesse de Bourbon, a daughter of Louis XIV and Madame de Montespan, and later enlarged several times. It was bought by Louis XV who wanted to bring it into line with the general architectural scheme of the Place de la Concorde (then Place Louis XV). In 1795 the interior was remodelled to accommodate the Chamber of the Five Hundred, and 1803–37 Napoleon commissioned Poyer to add on the neo-classical north front, as counterpart of the Madeleine. Under 'Restoration' rule the palace was returned to the Condé family, the last of the pre-Revolution owners, but in 1827 the State bought it back and made it the seat first of the Corps législatif, then of the Chambre des Députés. During the German occupation of 1940–44 the palace was used as the headquarters of the military administration of Greater Paris. After the Constitution of 1946 the Chambre des Députés became the seat of the Assemblée nationale.

47 The MADELEINE (here seen from the south-west) has a lively architectural history. The church construction undertaken by Constant d'Ivry in 1764 was, after his death in 1777, begun afresh by Couture who used new plans modelled on the Panthéon instead of the Dôme des Invalides. Work stopped at the outbreak of the Revolution but was taken up again in 1805 under Napoleon, who was planning a Temple of Fame for the soldiers of his *grande armée*. The task was given to Vignon who carried it out strictly in the style of the ancient classical temples. Louis XVIII finally decided that the building should serve its original purpose as a church, but it was not consecrated until 1842.

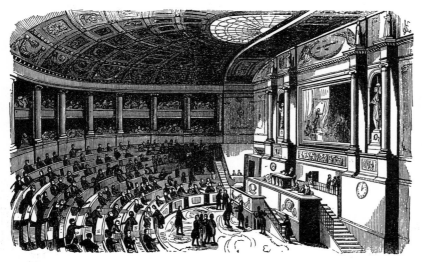

The Chambre des Députés

PLACE DE LA CONCORDE :
40 « LA RENOMMÉE »
41 « MERCURE »

43

42, 43 PLACE DE LA CONCORDE

44, 45 ARC DE TRIOMPHE

46
PALAIS
BOURBON

47
MADELE

Right Bank · Between the Opéra and the Louvre

48 Amid the bustle of a capital city, the CAFÉ DE LA PAIX by the Place de l'Opéra and the Boulevard des Capucines serves as the traditional meeting-place for foreigners. Behind is the ornamental façade of the Opéra.

49 Like a monumental back-drop for the northern end of the Place de l'Opéra, the elaborate façade of the grand opera-house (Académie nationale de Musique et de Danse) faces the Avenue de l'Opéra which leads to it from the Louvre. Begun in 1862 to the designs of Charles Garnier, this building, one of the most imposing products of the ostentation-loving Second Empire, was only finished in 1875, by

The Palais-Royal, after an engraving of 1778

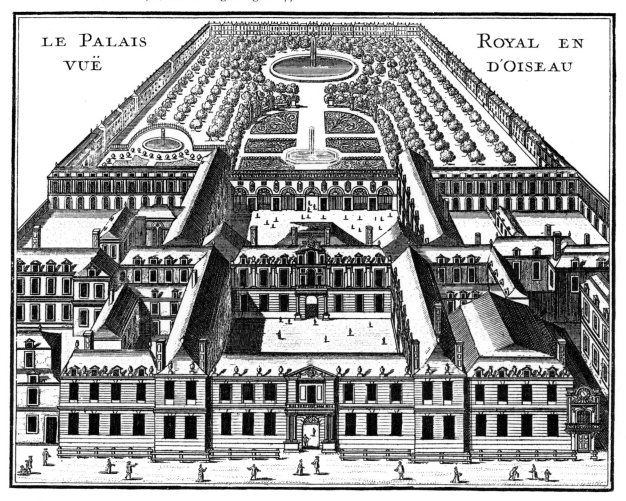

LE PALAIS VUË ROYAL EN D'OISEAU

which time the Third Republic had supervened. The great heyday of French opera, which for several decades had ensured the Paris stages a superiority in this field over all others in Europe, had, it is true, just then come to an end.

50 The THÉÂTRE-FRANÇAIS (Salle Richelieu), where the world-famous Comédie-Française, the leading theatre company of France, stage their plays. Designed by Victor Louis, it was added to the Palais-Royal (52) for Philippe Égalité in 1786–90. The State company of the Comédie, which for a time occupied the Odéon (62), finally settled here for good in 1790, since when it has fulfilled, with varying fortunes, the role of leading and most distinguished French-speaking theatre.

51 Set up in the foyer of the Théâtre-Français is the marble statue of the seated Voltaire, a masterpiece by Houdon of 1781.

52 The PALAIS-ROYAL was built by Jacques Lemercier for the Prime Minister, Cardinal Richelieu, who died there on 4 December 1642, leaving the 'Palais-Cardinal' to his royal master, Louis XIII. After the latter's death in 1643, it was taken over by Anne of Austria and her son, the young Louis XIV, and given its present name. Later the palace became the residence of the Duc d'Orléans, the King's brother, and his descendants. In 1781 Philippe Égalité built terraced houses round the garden, and the galleries on the ground floor were let to various merchants and dealers. During the Revolution the Palais-Royal became a centre of popular amusement and of political agitations. Used by the Bonapartes in the nineteenth century, it was set on fire during the Commune of 1871 and has, since its restoration, been the home of various State institutions. The photograph, taken from the Cour d'Honneur, shows the extensive gardens of the Palais-Royal seen through the gallery.

53 The PLACE VENDÔME, built by Jules Hardouin-Mansart in the reign of Louis XIV, on the site of the earlier Hôtel Vendôme, was originally designed to display an equestrian statue of the Sun King. During the Revolution this was replaced by a statue of Liberty and later, on Napoleon's orders, by the Vendôme Column. This, built in imitation of Trajan's Column, was topped by a statue of the Emperor in Roman dress. During the 1871 Commune the painter Courbet was responsible for having the column knocked down, but it was put up again in 1874.

54 The RUE DE RIVOLI was built 1806–35 alongside the Louvre and the Tuileries Gardens, and a row of houses with arcades and mansard roofs was put up on the north side by the architects Percier and Fontaine. By the Pavillon de Marsan in the Tuileries, the street broadens out into the Place des Pyramides, with at its centre Frémiet's gilded equestrian statue of Jeanne d'Arc, the goal of an annual procession on the day of the Saint's death.

55 In the BOULEVARD DE LA MADELEINE. This wide, elegant thoroughfare, one of the 'Grands Boulevards' at the centre of Paris life, came into being during the time of Louis XIV, when the wall which fortified the city to the north was replaced by an avenue. Under Napoleon III the network of boulevards, which formed the main arteries of the rapidly increasing traffic, was systematically extended.

PLACE DE
L'OPÉRA

VOLTAIRE.

52 PALAIS ROYAL

53 PLACE VENDÔME

54 PLACE DES PYRAMIDES

Left Bank · Latin Quarter · Montparnasse

Colour plate I (page 13). SAINT-GERMAIN-DES-PRÉS is the oldest church in Paris, with a nave and Romanesque tower dating mostly from the eleventh century. Both the abbey and the church were founded in the sixth century by the Merovingian king Childebert at the request of Bishop Germanus of Paris, and dedicated to Saint Vincent. Later they took on the name of Germanus whose miracle-working tomb was housed here. In medieval times the abbey became one of the most powerful in France. Our picture shows the view from the Boulevard Saint-Germain across the Place Saint-Germain-des-Prés, which, with its cafés, has today become a popular rendezvous for the intellectual and artistic *bohème* of the left bank.

56 The PANTHÉON: main front from the Rue Soufflot. In fulfilment of a vow made during a serious illness in 1744, Louis XV commissioned Jacques-Germain Soufflot to build a magnificent new church in place of the half-ruined abbey church of Sainte-Geneviève. Work was begun in 1758, and in spite of serious difficulties which arose in connection with founding and financing the church, it was almost completed by 1789.
In the pediment there is a relief by David d'Angers portraying the figure of the Motherland, flanked by Liberty and History, distributing wreaths among the meritorious.
The church was converted into a pantheon in honour of notable personalities in 1791; it reverted to the Church in 1806, was reconstituted as a Temple of Honour in 1830, was dedicated anew to Saint Geneviève in 1852, and concurrently with the burial of Victor Hugo in 1885 finally became a mausoleum for national heroes.

57 The church of SAINT-SULPICE, designed by Gamard and Gittard, was built after 1646 in place of a twelfth-century church which had served peasants attached to the abbey of Saint-Germain as a parish church. The neo-classical façade was executed by Servandoni (Jean-Nicolas Servan) in 1733. The interior, which was used as a victory temple during the Revolution, contains frescoes by Delacroix, and a famous organ.

58 SAINT-ÉTIENNE-DU-MONT is the church of Saint Genoveva (Geneviève), patron saint of Paris. It was founded in the thirteenth century as a parish church for servants and peasants attached to the abbey of Sainte-Geneviève, and rebuilt on a larger scale in 1491. The Renaissance façade dates from 1610–26.

59, 60 The entrance to the HÔTEL DE CLUNY on the Place Paul-Painlevé. The site, which was once covered with ruins of Roman *thermae*, became the property of the Benedictine monks of Cluny in 1340. Their Abbot built his Paris headquarters here and at the end of the fifteenth century these were given their present form as a magnificent Late Gothic (*style flamboyant*) palace. Since 1844 it has been a museum of antiquities.
The courtyard giving access to the main building is dominated by the projecting stair-tower.

61 View of the PLACE DE LA SORBONNE with the ÉGLISE DE LA SORBONNE, from the Boulevard Saint-Michel. The building of this domed church was undertaken by Lemercier, under the direction of Richelieu, in 1635; it was completed in 1642, the year of the great cardinal's death, and contains his tomb. In medieval times the theological Collegium Sorbonicum, founded by Robert de Sorbon, confessor to Saint Louis, became the principal seat of the world-famous University of Paris.

62 The ODÉON with its neo-classical pillared portico was built by Wailly and Peyre as a base for the Théâtre-Français. Following two fires, in 1807 and 1818, it had to be renovated, becoming among other things the stage for the great Talma's activities. Besides housing the more conservative Comédie-Française, transferred in 1790 to the Salle Richelieu (50), the Odéon has in more recent times, under directors like Antoine and Gémier, played an important role in furthering the French theatre, which from 1959 onwards Jean-Louis Barrault also took a hand in – until in May 1968 the students put an end to his activities by claiming the building for their debates.

63 The CARREFOUR RASPAIL, in the centre of Montparnasse, the district frequented by artists and writers; here Rodin's STATUE OF BALZAC was set up in 1939.

64 The PALAIS DU LUXEMBOURG (view of the south front across the garden) was built 1615–20 by Salomon de Brosse for Marie de' Medici, widow of Henry IV. After Napoleon's time it was enlarged to accommodate the Senate and other institutions, and since 1946 it has once again housed the Senate.

65 Where the Boulevard du Montparnasse intersects the Avenue de l'Observatoire stands the monument to MARSHAL NEY, one of Napoleon's most able army leaders. Rodin considered this statue, sculpted by François Rude in 1853, the best in Paris.

66 The RUE DE FURSTENBERG, so called after a late seventeenth-century abbot holding the rank of cardinal, occupies the site of the former abbey of Saint-Germain. In the small idyllic square the painter Delacroix had his studio (on the left of the picture), now preserved as a museum.

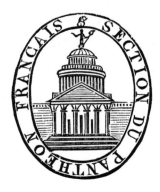

59

61

59 60 HÔTEL DE
CLUNY

61 ÉGLISE DE
SORBONNE

62 ODÉON

63 BOULEVAR
RASPAIL, B

64 PALAIS DU LUXEMBOURG

A LA MEMOIRE

DU MARECHAL NEY

DUC D'ELCHINGEN

PRINCE DE LA MOSKOWA

7 DECEMBRE 1853

66 RUE DE FURSTENBERG

Vâl-de-Grâce · Parks · Fountains · Barrières

67 The monastery of VAL-DE-GRÂCE in the Rue Saint-Jacques was founded by Queen Anne of Austria, wife of Louis XIII, who housed the Benedictines from Val-de-Grâce (Bièvres) here. The church in particular was built in fulfilment of a vow to commemorate the birth of her first son (Louis XIV). Work was begun in 1645 to the designs of François Mansart; the cupola was the work of Gabriel Le Duc after his return from Rome. The former monastery is now at the disposal of the Army Medical Corps.

68 Today still, in the JARDIN DU LUXEMBOURG (see also colour plate VIII), one can witness the delight of children riding the brightly painted animals of the old-fashioned merry-go-round, described by Rainer Maria Rilke at the beginning of the century in his poem *The Roundabout* with its refrain '. . . and every now and then an elephant all white'.

69 The PARC MONCEAU, situated in a fashionable quarter in the north-west, originated in the garden designed for Philippe Égalité by Carmontelle; in 1862 it was converted into a public park in the English style at the instigation of Napoleon III. The ornamental lake dates from the first period. The ivy-covered colonnade stems from the unfinished Rotonde which Catherine de' Medici wished to set up in Saint-Denis as mausoleum for Henry II.

70 The merry-go-round in the JARDIN DU LUXEMBOURG (68). The scene recalls Rilke's lines '. . . even a stag is there as in the forest,/ only he wears a saddle and upon it/ is strapped a little girl in blue.'

71 The BARRIÈRE SAINT-MARTIN, today usually referred to by the name of ROTONDE DE LA VILLETTE, at the Place Stalingrad, the former Rond-point de la Villette, was put up by Ledoux in 1789. The people came to regard it as a symbol of the hated *Fermiers généraux*; however, it survived arson at the time of the Commune of 1871 and now houses an archaeological museum.

72 One of the two *pavillons* of the BARRIÈRE D'ENFER by the Place Denfert-Rochereau of 1784. The erection of a toll-wall round the city by the architect Ledoux on the

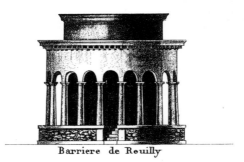

Barriere de Reuilly

instructions of the *Fermiers généraux* was one of the boldest undertakings of pre-Revolution Paris. This wall with its sentry-boxes enabled a strict control of all traffic to be maintained. Outside the wall, a wide boulevard with three avenues of trees formed the Chemin de Ronde. Where the approach roads entered, sixty *barrières* were set up for the collection of the *octroi* (city tolls). In the forty-three *barrières* he himself designed, which usually comprised a pair of *pavillons* on either side of the entrance-way, Ledoux gave expression to his own new brand of fancifully diversified constructional ideas deriving from classical antiquity. Unfortunately, the further expansion of the city during the nineteenth century has meant that only three of these *barrières* by Ledoux have remained intact (see 74 and also the drawings of *barrières* since pulled down on pages 24, 31, 111, 112, 132).

73 The PAVILLON DE CHARTRES at the entrance to the Parc Monceau (69) belongs to the buildings incorporated in Ledoux's toll-wall, but with its elegant pillared rotunda departs from the severe style of the genuine *barrières*.

74 The BARRIÈRE DU TRÔNE, erected by Ledoux in 1788, is situated close to where the Avenue du Trône runs into the Place de la Nation. Beside the two toll-buildings stand two columns, dominating the monumental approach to the city. The original PLACE DU TRÔNE was so designated to commemorate the throne set up in 1660 on the entry of Louis XIV; it was renamed Place du Trône-Renversée in 1793 and received its present name of PLACE DE LA NATION in 1880 on the occasion of the first celebration here of the national festival of 14 July. The statues of Philip Augustus and Saint Louis which crown the pillars were added in the reign of Louis-Philippe.

75 The monumental FONTAINE DES QUATRE-SAISONS interrupts the façade of the Rue de Grenelle next to the house where the poet Alfred de Musset lived 1824–40. The fountain portraying the figure of the City of Paris flanked by Seine and Marne, and decorated with reliefs of the four seasons, was executed 1739–46 by the sculptor Bouchardon.

76 The FONTAINE DES INNOCENTS in the centre of the Place des Innocents, a former market square, by the Rue Saint-Denis, is an attractive Renaissance monument erected in 1550 by Lescot and decorated with reliefs by the sculptor Goujon.

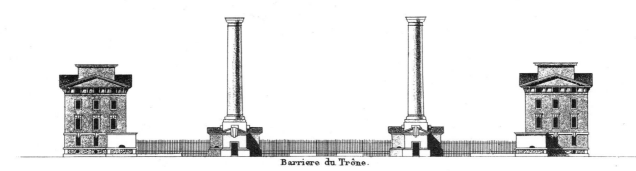

Barriere du Trône.

67

70 JARDIN DU LUXEMBOURG

71 ROTONDE

BARRIÈRE
D'ENFER

73

73 PARC MONCEAU, PAVILLON DE CHARTRES
74 BARRIÈRE DU TRÔNE

74

75 **FONTAINE DES QUATRE SAISONS**

76 **FONTAINE DES INNOCENTS**

Montmartre · Invalides · Porte Saint-Denis

77 A monumental stairway leads across the Square Saint-Pierre up to the BASILIQUE DU SACRÉ-CŒUR. This Romanesque-Byzantine edifice, built between 1876 and 1919 to the designs of Paul Abadie to commemorate the events of 1870, has, with its great white central dome, become one of the landmarks of Paris.

78 RUE CORTOT, one of the streets in old Montmartre, where many painters, writers and musicians have lived since the early nineteenth century. At No. 12 (on the right of the picture) the following lived in turn: Renoir, Émile Bernard (with whom Van Gogh and Gauguin associated), Maximilien Luce, Utter, Suzanne Valadon and her son Maurice Utrillo, Raoul Dufy, Othon Friesz.

79 RUE NORVINS by the Place du Tertre in old Montmartre. See also colour plate X showing the other entry to the Rue Norvins with the dome of Sacré-Cœur beyond.

80, 81 At the PLACE DU TERTRE, centre of the old rustic Montmartre. The 'Commune libre du vieux Montmartre', whose headquarters are here, is a modern association for safeguarding the popular traditions of this old artists' quarter. In the Square, with which Utrillo, Vivin and many others have familiarized us in their canvases, painters, graphic artists, portrait-painters, silhouette-cutters, provincials, parties of school-children and foreigners mingle to make a colourful scene.

82 The little Romanesque church of SAINT-PIERRE DE MONTMARTRE is all that remains of the mighty medieval Benedictine abbey of Montmartre, which was consecrated at Whitsuntide of the year 1147 by Pope Eugene III in the presence of King Louis VI.

83 RUE DU CALVAIRE, one of the sets of steps which lead up to the Butte Montmartre, over 300 ft above the Seine. The name Montmartre derives from 'Mont de Mercure', which tradition converted into 'Mont des Martyrs' in the eighth century. See also colour plate IX (page 39) showing the Rue Chappe.

84 The PALAIS DE LA LÉGION D'HONNEUR was built in 1782 by the architect Rousseau at the behest of the Prince of Salm-Kyrburg, who however ran into financial difficulties before its completion. In 1799 Madame de Staël and her husband, the Swedish ambassador, resided here, after which it came into the possession of Napoleon, who decreed that it should house the Legion of Honour. During the Commune of 1871 the palace was destroyed, but rebuilt in 1878. The side fronting the Seine, with its elegant pavilion, is in marked contrast to the severely classical pillared courtyard opening on to the Rue de Lille.

85 View of the north entrance of the HÔTEL DES INVALIDES. This vast edifice arose as the result of Louis XIV's epoch-making edict of 24 May 1670, which provided for better treatment of wounded soldiers. Built after plans by Libéral Bruant (1671–76), with corridors 10 miles long, it has room for 5,000 patients. In 1677 the work

was taken over and continued by Jules Hardouin-Mansart (see also colour plate IV). Today only a few war invalids live here, and the buildings house various military institutions and an army museum.

Colour plate IV (page 25). The DÔME DES INVALIDES, a masterpiece of architecture by Jules Hardouin-Mansart, who designed the great garden-front at Versailles and other Louis XIV buildings, took shape between 1679 and 1706. It fits into the south frontage of the Hôtel des Invalides like a great central jewel. The tall, lead-covered cupola is gilded and its topmost point is nearly 105 m. high. On 15 December 1840, Napoleon's coffin was taken to the Dôme des Invalides and in 1861 it was finally laid to rest in the tomb built by Visconti. The side chapels and crypts contain, among others, the tombs of Turenne, the Duke of Reichstadt (Napoleon II) and Marshal Foch.

86 The PORTE SAINT-DENIS, which stands at the junction of the Rue Saint-Denis and the Boulevards Saint-Denis/de Bonne Nouvelle, was built in 1672 to designs by François Blondel. It was put up by the city of Paris in honour of victories won by the armies of Louis XIV in Germany. The south face, reproduced here, shows reliefs executed by the brothers Anguier after designs by Girardon. These depict the Crossing of the Rhine and allegories of Holland and the Rhine.

Porte Saint-Martin;
engraving based on the work
of Bullet and Blondel, 1676

78

79

MONTMARTRE :
78 RUE CORTOT
79 RUE NORVIN

80 PLACE
DU TERTRE

86 PORTE SAINT-DENIS

The West · Along the Seine

87 View from the Eiffel Tower towards the south-east across the CHAMP-DE-MARS, the former parade-ground and scene of festive proceedings during the Revolution. At the far end of the open space stands the Ecole Militaire, built by J.-A. Gabriel 1751–56 as a military college for indigent members of the nobility; today it houses various institutions for advanced military training. In the middle distance, the UNESCO building (94) with its severe lines.

88 Begun in 1921, the CITÉ UNIVERSITAIRE has, thanks to generous endowments, grown up on what used to be fortified ground near the Porte d'Arcueil in the south of Paris, for the purpose of providing suitable quarters for the University students. The complex of buildings covers nearly 100 acres, and accommodates a steadily growing number of men and women students, including foreigners. Of the houses of the various nations, we show the FONDATION SUISSE, one of Le Corbusier's more controversial designs.

89 The ornamental cast-iron structures which Hector Guimard produced for the entrances to the MÉTRO, the Paris underground railway, at the turn of the century are a permanent reminder of the attempts of Art Nouveau to apply novel artistic forms to contemporary constructional requirements.

90 The BOIS DE BOULOGNE, formerly part of a forest (Forêt de Rouvre), was bequeathed to the city of Paris by the French State in 1852. With London's Hyde Park as pattern, it was converted into a public open space of 2,155 acres, with lakes, islands, fountains and avenues surrounded by magnificent trees.

91 The PONT ALEXANDRE III across the Seine dates from the turn of the century; its metal arch has a span of 107·5 metres. Tsar Nicholas II laid the foundation-stone of the bridge, named after his father and predecessor, in 1896 and it was completed in 1900. It follows the line running from the Dôme des Invalides (colour plate IV) across the Esplanade des Invalides and the Avenue Alexandre III to the Place Clemenceau in the Champs-Elysées. At the south end of the bridge and to the left of it stands the GRAND PALAIS (colour plate VII) built for the World Exhibition of 1900.

92 The bridge at Passy, known since 1949 as PONT DE BIR-HAKEIM, was built in 1906 as a road bridge with an iron viaduct above to carry the *Métro*.

93 The EIFFEL TOWER, viewed from the Champ-de-Mars, the capital's former army parade-ground. The huge iron structure was built by the firm of the engineer A.G. Eiffel to designs of the Swiss architect Maurice Koechlin for the Great Exhibition of 1889. Although many contemporary artists and writers – among them Verlaine – derided it, the Eiffel Tower became the popular emblem of modern Paris, and was for several decades the tallest building in the world.

94 The building erected for UNESCO (United Nations Educational, Scientific and Cultural Organization) between 1955 and 1958 to the designs of the architects Breuer, Nervi and Zehrfuss, has a number of artistic accessories contributed by various nations, including a Japanese stone-garden by Noguchi.

95 The PALAIS DES MUSÉES DE L'ART MODERNE between the Avenue du Président Wilson and the Avenue de New York beside the Seine, was built for the Great Exhibition of 1937 (architects: Dondel, Aubert, Viard and Dastugue). The two wings comprise a State Museum and a City Museum, which also serve to house various temporary exhibitions. The side facing the Seine contains a large relief by Janniot, and in the middle of the terrace stands a statue, 'La France', by Bourdelle, put up in 1948 in memory of those volunteers who died for their country in the Second World War.

96 In the Chaillot area, near the Trocadéro and its congeries of classical exhibition buildings, a new museum quarter has grown up in recent decades. The MUSÉE DES TRAVAUX PUBLICS, situated where the Avenue du Président Wilson joins the Avenue d'Iéna, was built in 1937–38 by Auguste Perret, and contains an interesting collection of technical exhibits.

97 View from the left bank of the Seine towards the PONT D'IÉNA, built 1809–13 by Lamandé and later repeatedly widened, which leads from the Square surrounding the Eiffel Tower to the terrace with the PALAIS DE CHAILLOT. The latter, designed by the architects Carlu, Boileau and Azéma, was built for the Exhibition of 1937 to replace the former Trocadéro, itself a product of the World Exhibition of 1878. The terrace is ornamented with sculptures by forty different artists.

98 The iron structure of the PONT DE GRENELLE dating from 1875 has recently been replaced by this graceful arched bridge of reinforced concrete. Beyond it, on the right bank of the Seine, can be seen the MAISON DE LA RADIO ET DE LA TÉLÉVISION, designed by M. Bernard.

Barriere de l'Ecole Militaire (*)

87, 88

89

94 MAISON DE L'UNESCO

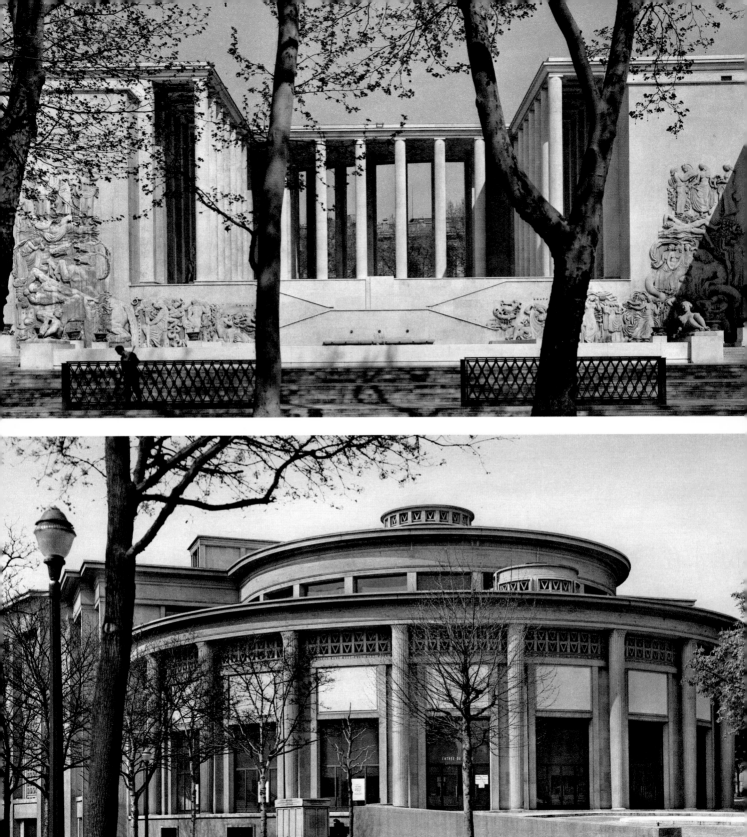

Chronology

53/52 BC: Caesar, in his *De bello Gallico*, refers to the town of Lutetia (=marsh) set on an island in the River Sequanae, and its inhabitants the Parisii.

The Roman city grows up round the hill of Sainte-Geneviève on the left bank of the Seine.

Saint Dionysius (Saint Denis), the first Bishop of Paris, is put to death in AD 285, according to tradition.

The inhabitants retreat to the islands in the river in the face of mounting barbarian invasions at the end of the third century.

292–306: The Roman Caesar Constantius Chlorus resides in Lutetia.

Flavius Claudius Julianus (Julian the Apostate), Roman Caesar (subsequently Emperor), sojourns in Paris 358 and 359–60, and writes in his *Misopogon*: 'Lutecia . . ., that is the name the Celts apply to the little town of the Parisians, situated on the river which surrounds it on all sides, so that one can only reach them from two sides across wooden bridges. . . .'

417–436: Saint Marcellus, Bishop of Paris.

508: The Merovingian Clovis I, appointed Consul by the Byzantine Emperor, after conversion to the Roman-Catholic Christian faith, makes Paris the capital of the Frankish Empire he has founded.

Saint Genoveva (Saint Geneviève, born *c*. 422 in Nanterre, died 512 in Paris), traditional founder of the church of Saint-Denis, is made patron saint of Paris.

861: Charles the Bald strengthens the fortifications of Paris.

885/86: Paris is successfully defended by Count Odo (Eudes) and Bishop Gozlin during a three-month-long siege by the Normans.

Hugo Capet, Count of Paris and King of the Franks since 987, founds the Capetian dynasty. His palace on the Cité island progressively extended by his successors.

Under Louis VI 'the Fat' (1108–37) the city's trading citizens combine to form a guild to control commercial traffic on the Seine.

1163: Pope Alexander III consecrates the new choir of Saint-Germain-des-Prés and at the invitation of Bishop Maurice de Sully couples with this the laying of the foundation-stone for the cathedral of Notre-Dame.

Under King Philip Augustus (1180–1223) the building of the Louvre as a royal palace is begun and numerous other building projects are put in hand. He has a new ring of fortifications built round the city, reconstitutes the Administration and in 1200 organizes the Paris schools to form a university.

97, 98

Under Louis IX (Saint Louis, 1226–70) the city makes further strides. He is responsible, among other things, for the building of the Cité palace. He appoints to the office of Provost (Prévôt des marchands), which had abused its overriding authority and fallen into disrepute through corruption, Etienne Boileau, 'the kingdom's most scrupulous judge', who gives the inhabitants a new sense of security. He it is who institutes the statute for the craftsmen's and merchants' guilds, which was not finally rescinded until the Great Revolution.

King Philip IV (Philippe le Bel, 1285–1314) makes Paris the seat of Parliament, that is, of the highest court of law in the kingdom, and installs it in the old palace on the Cité island.

Étienne Marcel, as Prévôt des marchands, wields practically unbridled power and provides the city with a new fortified wall. During the rising of 1357 he attempts to put the unrestricted municipal liberties into effect against feudal power but is defeated by a representative of the moderates in 1358.

Charles V ('the Wise', 1364–80) has the Bastille built and founds the Library which ultimately becomes the Bibliothèque Nationale.

1382: In March the Maillotins ('the men with the clubs') revolt against the excessive taxation. The following year Charles VI, under the direction of his uncle, is once again master of the situation and saddles the citizens with still more levies. Municipal self-government is suspended for several years.

The rivalry of the Dukes of Burgundy and Orleans is resolved through the murder of the latter in 1407. Whereupon the city suffers further unrest as a result of the struggle between the Cabochins, the adherents of Burgundy led by Simon Caboche, and those of Armagnac.

King Henry V of England, as son-in-law of Charles VI, enters Paris. Both kings die in 1422. On 8 September 1429 Jeanne d'Arc is wounded during an attack on the Saint-Honoré Gate. Henry VI of England, aged ten, is crowned King of France in Notre-Dame in 1431; the Duke of Bedford acts as Regent for the young King until 1435.

In November 1437 King Charles VII of France enters Paris.

Under Louis XI the first printing-press is started up in the Sorbonne in 1469.

The Renaissance King Francis I (1515–47), who resides mainly on the Loire, has part of the Louvre pulled down in order to make room for a more magnificent palace.

Catherine de' Medici, widow of Henry II who died in 1559, acts for a time as Regent for her sons. She has the Tuileries Palace built for her use. She is behind the massacre, on the night of 23–24 August (Saint Bartholomew's Day) 1572 of Admiral Coligny and countless other Protestants.

Between 1587 and 1591 the city defies the power of the sovereign when the 'Sixteen' set up by the sixteen city districts operates its strict regime.

On 22 March 1594 Henry IV of Navarre ('Paris is worth a Mass') enters the capital and resides in the Louvre until his murder in 1610. The Pont-Neuf dates from his reign. His widow Marie de' Medici has the Palais du Luxembourg built.

Louis XIII and his minister Richelieu are responsible, *inter alia*, for the creation of the royal printing-works (1610), the Jardin des Plantes (1626) and the French Academy (1635). The bishopric of Paris is separated from that of Sens in 1623 and elevated to an archbishopric.

During the minority of Louis XIV the nobility and citizens form the Paris Fronde, directed against the Queen-Mother Anne of Austria and Cardinal Mazarin.

During the reign of Louis XIV the city is further developed, particularly after Colbert has been put in charge of building works. Among the additions are the colonnades of the Louvre and the Dôme des Invalides. The King himself moves his Court to Versailles between 1678 and 1680.

Under Louis XV (1715–74) and Louis XVI (1774–93), who both reside at Versailles, Paris continues its uninterrupted growth; when in 1724 the number of its inhabitants approaches 400,000 a Minister remarks: 'Where the size Paris has now reached is concerned, no kind of further growth can be tolerated without sending the city to its doom.'

1784: A new wall with sixty *barrières* serving as toll-houses is erected round the city.

On 14 July 1789 the Great Revolution erupts with the storming of the Bastille. The last of the Prévôts des marchands is murdered, and Bailly takes charge of the newly constituted Mairie.

On 21 January 1793 the King is sent to the guillotine, a signal for the beginning of the Terror, during which countless heads roll on the Place de la Concorde.

On 18 Brumaire (9 November 1797) Napoleon Bonaparte assumes complete control, and on 2 December 1804 he has himself crowned Emperor in Notre-Dame in the presence of Pope Pius VII. Buildings symbolizing the Empire, such as the Madeleine in its role of a temple of victory and the Arc de Triomphe, are erected. The Louvre, declared a museum in 1793, is enriched with notable works of art.

On 30 March 1814 Paris surrenders to Napoleon's victorious adversaries. The occupation by the Allies is ratified on 30 May by the First Treaty of Paris. The Interregnum of the Hundred Days precedes the Second Treaty of Paris signed on 20 November 1814. The city's population now numbers 700,000.

During the Revolution of July 1820 barricades are set up for the first time. The 'bourgeois king' Louis-Philippe mounts the throne, Charles X having fled.

On 25 October 1836 the Obelisk from Luxor is erected in the Place de la Concorde.

During the Revolution of 1848 the Second Republic is proclaimed. In June of the same year General Cavagnac brutally crushes a rising on the part of the 'Fourth

Estate' of the workers. Prince Louis Bonaparte is elected President of the Republic on 10 December.

The edict of 2 December 1852, proclaiming Napoleon III Emperor of the French, following a plebiscite, initiates the epoch of the *Deuxième Empire* behind whose glittering façade all manner of new scientific and cultural forces gather strength. The focal point of the Great Exhibition of 1855 is the Palace of Industry. In 1859 the boundaries of the city are extended as far as the ring of fortifications; its area is thereby increased from 32 to 74.5 sq. km., the number of inhabitants from 1.2 to 1.8 million. Baron Haussmann, Prefect of the Départements Seine from 1853 to 1870, lays out the handsome boulevards.

In September 1870, following the Battle of Sedan, Paris is surrounded by German troops; it is shelled on 17 December. The city capitulates on 28 January 1871.

The rising of the Commune, March to May 1871, is suppressed by Marshal Mac-Mahon. Faced with the entry of the troops, the rebels shoot the hostages held by them, including the Archbishop of Paris, and attempt to destroy as many public buildings as possible by setting fire to them or blowing them up.

On 31 August 1871 Thiers is elected first President of the Third Republic.

The Exhibitions of 1878 (13 million visitors), 1889 (Eiffel Tower, 30 million visitors) and 1900 (51 million visitors) mark France's further advance into the Industrial Age; they confirm her role as international meeting-place and focal point of all the country's scientific and cultural potential.

In August 1914 the German armies advance upon Paris immediately after the outbreak of the First World War. The Government transfers to Bordeaux, and the Stock Exchange closes on 30 September. General Galliéni is made Gouverneur of Paris and calls upon its citizens to defend their capital. The Battle of the Marne having turned the tide, the Government returns on 10 December.

On 23 March 1918 the shelling of Paris by the long-range cannon 'Big Bertha' begins. On 11 November of that year the firing of maroons and the ringing of church bells signals the signing of the Armistice. In December the U.S. President Woodrow Wilson arrives, and 1919/20 the Paris Peace Conference is held.

A feature of the period 1918–39 is the 'merry-go-round' of Ministers and the resulting instability of the Third Republic's Administration.

The 'Arts décoratifs' Exhibition is held in 1925, the Colonial Exhibition in 1931, the World Exhibition 'Arts et Techniques' in 1937.

On 3 June 1940 an air raid by the German *Luftwaffe* brings to an end the 'phoney war' which had lasted eight months. With France no longer able to defend herself, Paris is declared an 'open city' on 14 June; shortly after, the capital is occupied by Hitler's troops.

A strike by the municipal workers of Paris on 15 August 1944 signals the overthrow of the German military regime; a general uprising follows on the 19th, and on the 24th the Leclerc Division reaches the suburbs. The following day the German Commandant of Greater Paris, General von Scholtitz, capitulates, having saved the city from major damage by ignoring Hitler's orders to destroy it first.

25 August 1944: De Gaulle returns to Paris amid universal rejoicing, and marches in triumph down the Champs-Elysées.

18 November 1944: Winston Churchill visits Paris. He and General de Gaulle lay wreaths on tomb of France's Unknown Soldier at the Arc de Triomphe.

January 1946 sees the beginning of the Fourth Republic when de Gaulle resigns as leader of the provisional government.

Autumn 1947: A nation-wide strike paralyzes the life of the capital.

8 July 1951: Paris officially celebrates the two-thousandth anniversary of its founding.

January 1959: De Gaulle, at the age of sixty-nine, is elected President of the Republic and instals himself in the Elysée Palace. Beginning of the Fifth Republic.

In 1966, under new measures promulgated by law, the Paris region is reorganized, the City of Paris becoming a separate new administrative unit.

May and June 1968: Student riots in Paris are followed by a wave of strikes which severely shake the administration.

27 April 1969: De Gaulle resigns as President, and is succeeded by Georges Pompidou.

10 November 1970: Charles de Gaulle dies. Heads of State and other distinguished mourners come from all over the world to attend a special memorial service in Notre-Dame two days later.

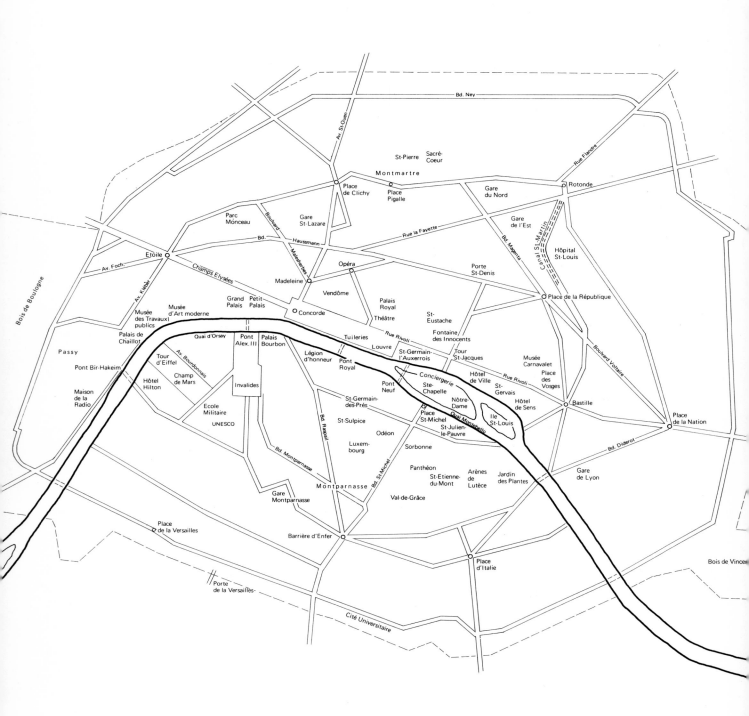

Bd. Ney

St-Pierre Sacré-
Coeur

Montmartre

Av. St-Ouen

Rue Flandre

Place
de Clichy

Place
Pigalle

Gare
du Nord

Rotonde

Parc
Monceau

Gare
St-Lazare

Boulevard

Gare
de l'Est

Rue la Fayette

Bd. Magenta

Canal St-Martin

Hôpital
St-Louis

Bd.

Haussmann

Opéra

Porte
St-Denis

Place de la République

Etoile

Av. Foch

Champs Elysées

Malesherbes

Madeleine

Vendôme

Palais
Royal

St-Eustache

Boulevard Voltaire

Av. Kléber

Grand
Palais

Petit
Palais

Concorde

Théâtre

Rue Rivoli

Fontaine
des Innocents

St-
Jacques

Musée
Carnavalet

Place
des
Vosges

Musée
d'Art moderne

Musée
des Travaux
publics

Tuileries

Rue Rivoli

Bois de Boulogne

Passy

Palais de
Chaillot

Quai d'Orsay

Pont
Alex. III

Palais
Bourbon

Légion
d'honneur

Louvre

St-Germain-
l'Auxerrois

Tour
St-Jacques

Bastille

Place
de la Nation

Tour
d'Eiffel

Pont Bir-Hakeim

Hôtel
Hilton

Av. Bourdonnais

Champ
de Mars

Invalides

Pont
Royal

Pont
Neuf

Conciergerie

Ste-
Chapelle

Nôtre-
Dame

Hôtel
de Ville

St-
Gervais

Hôtel
de Sens

Maison
de la
Radio

Ecole
Militaire

UNESCO

St-Germain-
des-Prés

St-Sulpice

Place
St-Michel

Quai Montebello

St-Julien-
le-Pauvre

Ile
St-Louis

Bd. Raspail

Odéon

Luxem-
bourg

Sorbonne

Bd. St-Michel

Panthéon

St-Etienne-
du-Mont

Arènes
de
Lutèce

Jardin
des Plantes

Gare
de Lyon

Bd. Montparnasse

Montparnasse

Val-de-Grâce

Bd. Diderot

Gare
Montparnasse

Place
de la Versailles

Barrière d'Enfer

Place
d'Italie

Bois de Vincen

Porte
de la Versailles

Cité Universitaire

Index of Plates